Humpty Dumpty America

HOW TO PUT AMERICA BACK TOGETHER AGAIN

United States Citizen

Copyright © 2019

ISBN: 9781794293861

TABLE OF CONTENTS

INTRODUCTION

AMERICA HAS CRUMBLED AND IS AMERICA NO MORE. Let's not be fooled by what is really going on.

This is not a book for political scholars; you know who you are and you are much smarter than I will ever be. This is a book for Americans who simply want to get America back! This book is for those individuals who are frustrated, walking around wondering what they should do or shouldn't do, what they should say or not say and those who are entirely confused and troubled about what has happened so quickly to America.

I am an American citizen and am here to tell you, sadly, that our country has fallen, cracked in thousands of pieces and we need to put it back together again before America is no more.

I have great confidence in telling you who will "not" be putting us back together.

It will not be Washington's brilliant politicians. It will not be the educators in kindergarten or at Harvard or the entertainers of the world with their great speeches at Hollywood events or the Media disguised as journalists or the football "activists," or the wildly wicked corporations throughout the world or even you and me.

It will be none of these because it will have to be all of these.

We're done. We're broken. We're at the *"I'm so low I have to rally to die"* moment.

I was *"kind of"* bothered (but not really) by all of this a few years ago but kept "turning the channels" because I really did not want to hear it. I was busy working every day, like you, paying my bills, getting my kid through college and trying to just "mind my own business."

The world was changing faster and faster and appeared to be on a wild down-hill spiral, going off the tracks of what used to be almost normal, but I kept telling myself that it was me "over exaggerating" again, because I have a tendency to do that anyway.

After all, the world's problems were not mine.

My problems were my problems and that was enough for me. Getting my energy bill paid was my problem, figuring out student loans and how to pay them back was my problem, hiding gauze in my cheekbone to lessen the pain of a broken tooth was my problem, finding out who had the best sales at the grocery store was my problem, or figuring out if a new fuel pump for "Betsy" was more cost effective than a newer car; those were my problems but certainly not the world slipping away from me.

I would take care of the situations around these 4 walls and the "leaders" would have to take care of the rest. After all, my "leaders" were the ones in charge, the ones who cared about me and my country and I would just wait for the remedies of a confusing mixed-up America to come forward to clear up this mess with brilliant decision-makers, savvy lawyers and politicians and I would keep moving forward with my own life.

And then the noise became louder and louder and I couldn't turn the channels anymore and I started getting sad and then frustrated and then angry and then more angry and then very *very* angry because I could see very clearly and didn't like what I was seeing. I was actually quite scared.

I could hear America banging its head against the wall every day getting sicker and sicker, looking dramatically different in such a short time and while I did need to deal with toothaches and student loans, I probably needed to be accountable beyond my 4 walls because this is my America too and something very wrong was happening to all of us!

I am part of this family and I don't want to lose what people have fought so hard for me to have.

And here we are in 2019, at war with one another and the chaos is quietly getting louder and louder each day.

PART I

WASHINGTON DC

"Let's get the hell out of here; I'm starving. Do you want to meet me at Joe's? I've been up since 5 am and I really need to unwind and a Scotch or three should do the trick. These nitwits aren't moving and I'm sick of looking at them."

"I hear yah. Joe's sounds perfect. I'll have my car pick you up in 30 minutes. Will you be ready? I just need to make a quick stop and I should be there. I'm picking up the cigars from Sammi first. Be prepared to be amazed, my friend. You'll get some; don't worry.

Don't let me forget to tell you about my meeting with Lex. I saw him at the gym and he did confirm the sale is taking place; I think we need to make our move before the 15th. The news will be out on the 18 th so the timing will look good for us but I will talk to you about it when I see you but I think it's going to be a pretty sweet deal. See you in a bit."

<u>Dear Washington DC</u>: We are "your" bosses and you are not "our" Rulers. I would like to tell you first and foremost, Democrats, Republicans, Libertarians and anyone else with a job there, that you've all failed us. You've more than failed us. I can't even describe what scum-buckets you really are and that's about 95% of you. Probably more like 98%.

There will be new rules in place for you and it's not going to be pretty but what you've done to us is not so pretty either.

In no special order, these are the new rules and what has to be done if we are to get America back.

A. TERM LIMITS

To the House of Representatives & Senators-Wow!

What a ride you've had. How wonderful it must be, living in your pretend state with your elite zip codes; your oasis from reality. The rules are changing. They have to. We cannot continue this downward spiral.

There will no longer be unlimited 2 and 4, or 6 year terms for you. The people have spoken. You will be able to stay in Washington for a period of no longer than 4 years. That is non-negotiable. You "can" stay in Washington all your life if you choose to but no longer as a senator or congressman and no longer on our dime!

B. SALARIES

Your salaries are being reduced. They are too high and the "surf n turf" days will be ended at the end of your term. You will also not be controlling your "raises" and "benefit packages" from this moment on.

You will never be able to touch a Bill that decides what you can and cannot take from us anymore. That's rude, disrespectful, arrogant and wildly stupid and irresponsible. We the people acknowledge this gross error by allowing it to happen for so long but we are now taking care of it.

We will vote on your salaries every 4 years. You work approximately 140 days a year? You will be paid accordingly.

C. JOB DESCRIPTION

During your stay in Washington, you will actually need to work and complete your job. You need to actually "be there" to vote and to get your tasks "checked off" before you head out of town. If there is a government shutdown then, you too, will not be paid.

You will also no longer be allowed to take any trips paid for by taxpayers and/or lobbyists. You will need to just "stay put" and do your job until issues are resolved. There have been way too many "recesses" for you. Recess is now over.

The vote called "Present" will no longer be an option. You need to put you "big boy pants" and "big girls pants" on and make a decision. You're not getting paid to be "Present." If that was the case, we could get some dogs and cats and mice and a few rats in there and they could vote "Present."

If you do not vote and choose to simply be "Present," the government will deduct 5% for each vote you miss or make as "Present." If there are health issues or extenuating circumstances you will need to bring proof as to why you were not there to vote. The 5% taken will be 5% of your gross pay that is deducted.

With these new rules in place, it should be much simpler for you to keep your heads on straight and to actually work for the people that hired you, now that you know you are only there for 4 years. True leaders might actually come to the forefront and start shining on America.

What does Washington know and when do they know it?

How did so many of you go to Washington as "good old middle class folk" and come out millionaires? I marvel at the insider trading you do and the pretty suits and town cars that take you to work, to the club, to the bar, to the oyster shop, to the hotels and the lifestyle that you apparently feel so entitled to.

We're watching you now. We're not doing it secretly; we're not doing it via a democrat or republican or libertarian leader but rather with clear transparency by the people. These employees will be hired to watch you and we will make sure they, too, have no political agendas. They will simply make sure that our new rule of order for our "leaders" is followed and taken seriously.

D. INSIDER TRADING

Hold your breath you clever ocean-side dirty dogs because there is no more "insider trading" for you! That's stopping today. We do know that this is just one of several legal ways, loopholes that have allowed so many of you to come out millionaires. That practice is over. You have made too many decisions in your special committees based on alga-rhythms called: "*how is that going to benefit me and oh boy my gold chips are coming in soon*" and you have been way too "*hilliaryish*" and it's over. You have no more access to information that will line your pockets. If you or any member of your family do a deal with the devil, you and said family member will go to prison just like everyone else. It will not be a federal prison with tennis courts and luxury styles of the "rich and famous," kind of prison because we are closing them down as well.

Please know that you can no longer do any trading or have any involvement with any companies that you've been associated with during your government position. In fact, those committees you are on will have our "watch dogs" in your bank accounts for the duration of your term and 1 year after you leave Washington.

E. HOUSING

As public servants of this country, your housing options will be changing as well. We the people would be better served if our public servants lived in apartments "dormitory style," for the few years that you are in Washington. It is better this way. You will have to learn to get along with one another, just like you want us to get along with one another.

You are not there to be waited on by servants or march around like you are multi-millionaires. It will hurt for a while but you will get used to it; the people that should be there will be there; the people there for the wrong reasons will run away as fast as they can. We look forward to watching you run.

We are tired of our public servants losing perspective about the states they represent and the country they are called upon to serve, that being the United States of America. It is a very important short term assignment; do good work and then go home.

F. NEEDS vs. WANTS

How many employees do you really need?

We are cutting our overhead here. Senators and Congressmen will no longer have 18 or even more than 18 full time employees under them while they are serving the people. You will now have the opportunity to hire 5 employees for the duration of your stay. You can also solicit free internships if you choose but that would be your responsibility and the government will not fund your interns.

We are excited to inform America that this will result in saving millions of dollars for the tax payers!

Furnishing your office should not be a wild spending spree. You are no longer getting up to $40,000 allowance for furniture and you are not getting any kind of an allowance for extra office space. This has been another absurd "gimme gimme" and a wild and reckless waste of funds. You will get a $5,000 allowance and you will have to provide receipts. The receipts will have to be for your office, truly, not your "home away from home" apartment, not for your lover, not for your friends and family. This allowance is only for your office. We will keep it at $5,000 for now but will consider lowering it later on. I'm assuming you already have a desk in your office. Really, what else do you need? If you do need more items than this allowance will provide, then you can go to the Salvation Army or the Goodwill or any local thrift shops. Remember those places? They are incredible. You will be helping members in the community. You can stain your furniture and sand it or hire someone looking for work. I'm sure you have contacts.

G. HEALTH CARE

What in the hell is wrong with you? You don't get *"special health care."* You get the same crap you shoved down our throats and told us to take it or else. You know… the deal that you didn't have time to read but needed to sign it so you *could* then read it? Yah… that deal! You also don't get up to 70% assistance in paying your premiums. When your job is over in Washington, you don't keep getting your insurance either. You're not a hero like a VET or something. You're a public servant. By you doing a 2-4 year job does not entitle you to life time health care. It also does not entitle you to lifetime retirement. You have the same retirement rules in effect as everyone else. Try to figure out the rules from the IRS. Good luck with that!

H. LOBBYISTS

Goodbye for good. How gross. This is probably one of THE grossest parts of accepted government behavior today. If we even try to follow the money trail it would most likely make us dizzy. It may have started as early as the 1800's but it has become a brilliant way to participate in bribery and extortion on a legal platform but this practice will cease immediately.

The largest spenders for this grotesque practice have been corporations. They have spent more than 2.5 billion every year to influence our law makers. Most large corporations today have at least 100 lobbyists working for them. The largest lobbyist group has been the US Chamber of Commerce, which I find absolutely amazing. You can probably follow the money and understand why the US Chamber of Commerce has had so much interest in sleeping with decision-makers.

Say goodbye to the mob-firms that hire nothing but lobbyists to rally full time and shove their agendas down politicians' throats. They, in turn, have shoved that crap down our throats and they walk away with their gold-lined pockets again. What a lovely world this will be without the lobbyists and politicians sleeping together in such a dirty bed.

We the people will be very relieved to see you gone.

I. YOUR SECRET SEX LIFE

We are not responsible to pay for your affairs anymore, hiding them and paying off the people you slept with. That's on you.

Last count there were 260-264 pay-offs and different sources state it is in the millions. Whether it's $1 or $1,000,000 or $25,000,000, you can pay for your own dirty clean-up jobs.

We will be publicizing those names and you will need to pay back that money. We will give you a lower interest rate if you need to make payments but it will not be lower than the interest rate that the government charges for student loans. It will be within that range or 1-2 points higher. Try not to worry; your significant others probably know the "true you" anyway and you won't be running for office again so you don't need to worry about your reputation being tarnished.

PART II

THE BUDGET

One of the easiest ways to cut the budget immediately without a 10 year debate would be for each department to review what they pay out every year.

A. UTILITIES

Each state and each department and each manager shall look at their monthly heating and cooling bill, and try to find ways to save money on utilities.

Every government building I am in during the summer is almost "chilly." I think you have your AC on 68-69? You might consider cranking that up to at least 72, which will save your department budgets thousands of dollars annually. The same goes for winter months. You need to make sure you turn the heat down at night and you don't need it at 75 during the day.

B. JOB DESCRIPTIONS

Employee hours and number of employees in each department needs to be looked at very closely. Each manager will review job descriptions and see if they (managers as well as employees) can take on 5-10% more work and that could easily remove hundreds of government positions.

C. TRAVEL

Travel points? No, they don't go to the employee or the employee's family anymore. You need to return them to your department. Your department will use those credits for future work-related travel. You did not pay for the ticket and you should not get the benefit of free travel.

No government employee shall be able to sit in First Class.

Management will also look into webinars. They are a good option for saving the country money, while still having effective meetings. We can save millions on travel participating in webinars.

D. VENDORS

Each manager will review all of the vendors they presently use and will research other opportunities to match or save money.

Management will spend time negotiating prices. They will participate in plans that give points back for more free products. This will take a little more time initially but you will save thousands of dollars annually. The country will save millions. You need to review not only the big ticket items but everything from toilet paper to printers.

E. GRANTS

We need to seriously revisit our Grants and Special Programs, every single one of them. This includes special grants like "trying to understand what bugs do when they are near a light," or "bird watching." I know I have had many a sleepless night wondering what the bug does and why he runs for the light but that query will have to be dealt with on my own time and not the government's. There are thousands and thousands of more absurd grants that are a total waste of money.

Imagine if all that money we spent on absurd ridiculousness was spent on something honest and worthy like true cancer research and not research to buy buildings but true research to beat cancer or Alzheimer's or any other awful disease.

We would still be able to save billions of dollars because we will be getting rid of the "junk" grants and supporting grants that could save lives, resulting in healthier citizens and less money spent on Medicare, Medicaid, etc.

This will be a "win win" for decades to come.

F. OUTSOURCING

There is no need to continually outsource on the state and federal level. Generally speaking, private companies charge more for the task than a federal employee would be paid.

Outsourcing has become outrageous. Management typically gets a task force or hires an outside company to "research" the possibilities and then moves forward. Millions and billions of dollars are wasted. Thousands to millions of dollars can be spent simply on the task force itself. After their reports come in, they then move forward with what they were most likely going to do in the first place but the "task force" gives them validity. We will now look internally and when doing "new hires," consider dual-tasking like the private sector.

G. ENTITLEMENT PROGRAMS

Each Senator and Congressman will be responsible for reporting back to their states exactly how much is spent on illegal aliens from SNAP to extra teaching to housing to insurance benefits.

Taxpayers deserve to know and they need to know where their money is going on a state wide basis. States will also need to publicize the "matching federal funds" they are receiving and those funds will start being reduced as well in order to reduce our deficit.

There is really no such thing as a Grant or Free Money. In the end, we the taxpayers are paying for it and we no longer can afford this reckless behavior.

Per www.howmuch.net, these are the the ten states most heavily weighed by the cost of illegal immigration. It is important to note that this does NOT include the Federal funds that are given to each state:

1. California – $23,038,125,353

2. Texas – $10,994,614,550

3. New York – $7,489,141,357

4. Florida – $6,290,429,108

5. New Jersey – $4,466,838,574

6. Illinois – $3,220,767,517

7. Georgia – $2,487,719,503

8. North Carolina – $2,437,965,113

9. Maryland – $2,378,996,947

10. Arizona – $2,314,131,964

"Kumbaya" programs cost billions of dollars (as shown on illustration) and they are not feasible simply because it is a good idea and we want to do good for others. It should be "family first" and this family is America.

Most sane people do not "borrow" money to go and then help someone else. Most "sane" people reach out and help others when they can, when they have taken care of their family first and then find it in their hearts to help others.

America is full of kind people who want to help but America needs to take care of America. It's not "racist" behavior to take care of your family; it's just common sense. It's not "racist" to say you cannot borrow and borrow to help another nation when you don't have the money to do it; it's just common sense.

This can reduce the deficit dramatically within a few years.

H. ILLEGAL WORKERS

It isn't simply a matter of letting someone come into the country and work. They may be working for cash or lower wages but once you count up the benefit package from the United States of America, they are doing quite well.

How amazing is it that someone in the US cannot afford health care anymore due to the high premiums but an illegal alien can obtain free health care? Isn't it amazing how they can also get free education? Isn't it amazing how they get energy assistance? That is not racism or bias but rather simple fact. You can shout "racism" all day long so we Americans will "shut down" in fear of being judged wrongly but we cannot be quiet anymore.

There is a "worker program" in place. This is a fabulous idea for our country as well as the hard workers coming in but these workers should still not be given free benefits. If there are here working legally, that's great! But with that privilege, they also need to realize that we are not responsible for educating their children, paying their health care or any other living expenses.

When we have the funds to help and when they are not borrowed funds, rest assured we will help but we cannot go into more debt and give less to America and more to illegal aliens. That is simply wrong.

PART III

EDUCATION

"Hi honey; I was wondering if you could go to that PTA meeting tonight. I'm really tired and I have to do a double tomorrow and I'm ready running late and need to get Tony to soccer. "

"Oh come on, don't do that to me. I don't really give a dam to be honest with you. I don't care what textbooks they are buying. That's not our job is it? Sounds like a bunch of political bureaucratic bullshit to me; seriously. I think it's ridiculous. Who's the idiot that started this anyway?"

"Come on, you know who did it. Rose started this two years ago and she's clearly not an idiot. I guess it just caught on and I think it's probably a good idea that parents are getting involved; I get it. We need to do something! For god's sake, they're brainwashing our kids and they're turning into little entitled monsters. Don't you want them to respect you serving and respect us as adults and respect us as a family? They're really doing a number on our kids and I don't want them changing like that. I saw some of his homework. It's nuts. By the time Sarah starts school, who knows what in the hell they will be teaching them. You know I'm right and I know you're tired; I'm tired too. I'd like to stop and get a pizza after soccer and then let's both go. I can ask my mom to come over. Come on, it's important."

"Fine but I'm not staying past 10 —I'm serious. I'll be home by 5. I agree. I'm just tired. See you soon."

A. JOB DESCRIPTION

The duty of an educator is to educate a specific topic. The duty of a teacher does not include brainwashing your child and vomiting political and religious opinions on them, unless of course you are in a private school, in which a specific religion and ideology is agreed upon before enrollment.

Public education needs to be transformed from the bottom up. What happened to these "educators" in our country? When did you turn the switch or was it just a gradual brainwashing for you as well?

What happened to the parents who forgot to get involved? Didn't you see the materials your children were bringing home? Did you think it was odd that they were changing little by little getting coached on a daily basis to hate America?

B. WHO WE EDUCATE

We educate citizens in this country. Our education will be taught in English and learned by those who speak English. This country has a deluge of programs for those children with learning disabilities but not being able to speak English should be considered a disability. States have the responsibility to continue taking care of the children with special needs and that funding is expensive. We shall not cut corners on special needs citizens in this country.

If a state chooses to help children learn our language, there should be a cost attached. The participation of this should also be done in the evening or after school, not during regular school hours. Parents of children that cannot speak or read English will also have to pay either in fees or labor. I'm sorry it doesn't come free; we simply don't have the extra money sitting in our piggy bank and we also cannot "dummie-down" our education anymore so the non-speaking English students can catch up.

There are jobs in municipalities that can be done, which will save the District money and then your children will have the opportunity to be in a classroom where they can properly learn the English language.

The other alternative is learning English before you come here. There are some cases when individuals are truly here to be out of harm's way and in those cases they cannot learn the language before they arrive but they will still be required to pay for this service.

Regardless of where you came from and why, you need to understand that education is a privilege and one that should be taken seriously by everyone.

C. TEACHING MATERIALS

Teachers and communities need to start working together honestly. That includes disclosure for materials that are being taught to our children.

We cannot allow educators to brainwash our children anymore. Educators need to step down from their arrogant pedestal, do a reality check as to why they are there and decide if teaching is really what they want to do.

If they want to be a political activist, that's great! You can be a political activist but please leave your badge at the Principal's office and get the hell out of there. America has had enough teacher-wacko-activists from kindergarten to graduate school.

These "teacher" activists are becoming traitors to our country. ***Shame on you***. You forgot to read the job description.

All lesson plans will be open for community members to review at any time. You will have to leave your political agendas at home.

D. BUDGET

There will be a review and update on budgets on an annual basis. There will be full transparency with regard to what you are spending all your dollars on. Like the federal offices, you will be mandated to do the same as far as building utilities and cutting costs in all departments and buildings.

Members in the community will be able to review your budget annually.

E. TENURE

That was another "good while it lasted" deal and will be deleted from kindergarten to university professors. There are so many reasons that this has not worked in the past, protecting the educators that should truly not be there, leaving out the good educators that cannot come in and totally neglecting the true needs of the student.

Tenure is a large part of our problem in schools today.

F. DISCLOSURES

Students need to be educated on their majors and minors in higher education and their career potential or lack thereof. The "White Men Suck" classes might be fun and great comradery for man-haters but for the 3-4-5 credits they are getting and the thousands of dollars the class itself costs, students should know where it is taking them, which is "nowhere" 99% of the time with regard to career choices and opportunities.

G. UNIONS

Teacher unions need to be revisited as well as their purpose and what is allowed and not allowed. Unions should no longer be mandated and members should have the right to opt out of them.

In 2018, there was over 3.8 million dollars spent on lobbyists for teachers unions. There the lobbyists go again! That will need to end as well. As stated above, when we get rid of lobbyists completely, the world will clearly be a better place.

When there are layoffs in schools, it is often times the "good teachers" that hit the road. That will need to change. I'm not sure who can change it in a fair manner but it certainly cannot be union rules. That is not working. It would be beneficial if local communities started getting more involved in voting on this process and how they wanted their communities to hire and lay off. After all, it is the community taxpayers funding the schools.

PART IV

PC
"POISON IVY RUNS WILD"

A. BACKGROUND

Contagious and nasty. Political correctness is one of the largest culprits attributing in America crumbling today. The popularity of being politically correct started sometime in the 80's and has taken over reality for the media, politicians, entertainers, schools, and even football players and a few stupid cheerleaders.

It's become the norm in our country, shoving it down the throats of children in school of all ages, human resources so corporations are scared straight to absurd new policies, sadly stinking up the churches so Priests and Ministers have forgotten what they are supposed to be doing at the pulpit, parents who want to fit in with the other goof-ball parents so they all hop on the "stupid parent train," to be accepted, the media, who told the true journalists to get the hell out of the building because true reporting is a concept of the past, moving forward with their own agendas, entertainers who are so completely righteous and fraudulent and self-serving, letting all of us know when they do something good so they can get credit while the puppets watch with "oohs and aaaahs," admiring them while they live in their secluded neighborhoods with fences and walls and kick-ass security, telling us to accept what they never could because they somehow know better and sure as hell deserve better, and our government who can't stand up straight and look us in the eye without some lies blurting out of their mouths and no backbone to stand up for people of this country because they have too much at stake for themselves.

What happened to you people?

Accepting someone for what and who they are is one thing but shoving it down our throat and being so "over the top" fragile is beyond ridiculous.

What happened to you college students who fought for free speech but the minute the agenda doesn't fit *your* free speech, you shove the vile naysayers off the curb.

Vagina hats? Come on now girls, now you're just embarrassing yourselves. I'm a woman and if that's the new deal, I'm out. I would be ashamed to be any part of this kind of absurd behavior. You give women a bad name. Surely, there must be a better way, a more effective way to express yourselves. Your family must be so proud of you ranting the streets like crazy people leaving your "classy self" at home, tucked away in the closet for no one to see.

B. THE NEW PLAN

How do we stop this wild fire? We stop it by stopping the nonsense immediately. We cannot and should not include every single "*uniqueness*" in our laws.

There is a man's bathroom and a woman's bathroom. It's really simple. If you are a man (but feel like a woman and/or dressed like a woman) you're still a man according to the bathroom rules. Go to the man's bathroom.

Same with women.

People are very understanding and I'm sure it will be accepted in a relatively short period of time. Back to basics.

If you feel like you are a horse, should we get a "horse bathroom" for you? If you think you are a chipmunk, should we get special "chipmunk huts" at the rest stops for you? If you feel like you are half man and half woman, should we get a private bathroom for you? If you get your feelings hurt in college, should we have special rooms for you paid by tax dollars where you can go and sob like a baby? If we get those rooms, how about the rooms for the students that aren't crying? Wouldn't it be only fair to give them "special rooms" because they're feeling good and maybe give them free beer or money or something to show our appreciation? Should we bring in special counselors so you can really "get into it" and cry your dam eyes out and then demand an "A" on all your missed classes because you were so conflicted or sad or just not feeling it? If you are a special religion, should we give you 5 breaks during the day to pray? If you are an atheist, should we give you 5 breaks a day to go outside and solicit your beliefs on the street corner? If you are Catholic, shouldn't you at least get off Friday mornings to attend Mass? If you are a white man, should you have your own bathroom far **FAR** away from everyone because you are just so dam evil?

See how stupid this is and how stupid it can get? It can go on and on and on. You could probably think of 50 examples right now that we could spend millions of dollars on.

This stops immediately. It has to. It is destroying us.

We can't change laws every 5 minutes to accommodate uniqueness. There are laws in place and I'm sorry if they don't match what you stand for but you're just going to have to deal with it. If you can't deal with it, then go to Mexico or Cuba or Sweden or some other area where you think life is pretty and free. Maybe they have the funds available to tolerate your personal "preferences" in life in the form of new laws.

We don't!

You could also review your "uniqueness" and take it for what it is and allow it to be yours and not ours.

We can no longer look back in history and retract symbols or heroes because one group or another does not agree with them or feels "uncomfortable" or "left out." Everything in our lives and in our country is not fair; it's not supposed to be fair and equal; it can't be.

PART V

THE MEDIA

"I've got a source from a source and it's a good source."

"But is it solid? Have you fact-checked it yet? "

"I'm just about done with that."

A. THE WILD WILD WEST

Welcome to the "Wild Wild West" of the media! They are very much like the fellow on the street corner selling Rolexes for $19.99 all day long.

> *"Oh Miss, you are going to love this Rolex. It is truly the real deal. I was in Switzerland on the day the factory went wild. I believe they produce only 2,000 fine watches a day but for some reason this day was unique. Management was visiting and the employees felt it would look good for them if they ramped up the factory line. It would show off how hard they have worked for this company. It was truly amazing. What was more amazing was that I was there. I was visiting friends, eating chocolate and quietly enjoying my day when I was approached by my cousin's friend who is in sales. It was that day that I was so blessed with these watches. Because they made too many on this one day, this one day that I was visiting, I was given these watches and told to never speak a word about the production error. You see, if the public knew, they would perhaps feel that pristine care was not given to the manufacturing of this very fine item. And for this reason and this reason only, I am able to share with you this very fine watch at such a discounted price. I could ask for much more money and I could get it but I feel it would be wrong. I feel good sharing it at this price for you today. It is my pleasure to offer you this*

beautiful Rolex at the incredible unbelievable price $19.99."

The media's job appears to be nothing but a continual day to day manipulation of story lines with a seeming objective of controlling how we vote, how we live, who we love and who we hate, who we can blame for our problems and who we can thank for our wins. The days end with us no longer being able to think for ourselves.

The days of true fact-checking are gone.

The internet has its own political agendas and will share with you the news they choose to share. Political bias is smeared on their faces every day. This has been another win for controlling America's thinking by those who want to take control.

B. ACCOUNTABILITY

This will start today. There are laws in place for libel and slander and there is also free speech.

If there are news reports that have not been vetted, there will have to be disclaimers that this is "opinion only" and not "true news." We will start fining networks as well as the internet. The excuse of: "I can't disclose my source," has become a rationale for false reporting.

Welcome to the new world of disclaimers.

It is important that we allow for free speech but it is also important to separate facts from opinion. When people work all day and come home to have supper and watch a little news, they believe they are watching "news" and not opinions. If the journalists choose to remain political activists, then they will have to rename their programming as such.

They will get one warning and then the fines will begin.

If they call themselves "journalists," they need to act as "journalists." If they portray themselves as "reporters," they need to be "reporting," and keeping opinions off the table. They will be allowed an "opinion" section of the news but it will be labelled clearly that it is the "opinion section" of the newscast.

America needs to get the true picture. Brainwashing stops today. Tired Americans that work all day don't come home and "fact-check" your "news" stories. They just assume you are speaking the truth.

We cannot "run the story" and then make a small retraction a week or so later. Clearly, the people doing this know that the damage has been done. Making a small retraction is hardly a price to pay for damaging someone's life. The fines will be attached to the reporter as well as the station representing the reporter. This will also be in effect to other outlets of media including but not limited to Facebook, Google, Twitter and Instagram. Full disclosure in bold and underlined will be before and after the "story lines" as opinion spots and not "news stories."

PART VI

SUMMARY

Our country is changing too fast and not for the good. It's hard to say if this was accidental or just a brilliantly thought-out plan from some underground network with deep pockets but here we are, 2019, and we need to decide what kind of a country we want to live in and we need to do it pretty dam quick.

I'm tired at the end of the day too. I have to work and I have just so many hours in the day, probably like you. I would like to shut my eyes and pretend this is just going to go away but, sadly, I don't think it will unless we all start a movement upward.

I will take small steps but hopefully ones that will start to make a difference.

My Pledge to America

I will call my representatives as much as I don't want to because most of them make me sick to my stomach and I feel like I'm just wasting time but I will do it. I will demand that they hear me and listen to my concerns. I will continually try to make them accountable.

I will keep talking when someone tries to shut me up and tells me I'm just a racist and I don't have the right to say what I'm thinking because I know I'm not a racist; I know I'm a good person and I'm a fair person and it has nothing to do with racism or discrimination. That tactic needs to stop. We can make it stop!

I will vote on every election. If I'm tired or the roads are bad or I just don't feel like it, I will still do it. I will tell everyone I know to vote as well. If there is a small election in my area, I will educate myself on the candidates and know who the person is when I start making those "check marks."

I will attend local government meetings, public hearings and especially school meetings, even though I no longer have kids in school. I will do it because I know it needs to be done and I am looking at America personally now and I'm taking this very serious. The children that go to school are part of my family. I want them to be safe on the bus, I want them to have fun and I want them to learn the good things about my country and I want them to be able to celebrate Christmas, Hanukah or any other celebration they want. I want them to be able to *not* celebrate if they so choose. I want them to say the Pledge of Allegiance and know why we honor our country. I want them to know what the words actually mean.

I will try very hard to listen to other viewpoints, even if they are wildly different from mine because I know we have to come together and I cannot shut those people down because I don't want them to shut me down when I am trying to express myself.

We cannot allow just one sector or another sector to make the change; they all have to change because they've all been poisoned and transformed into an America we weren't planning on. The picture is dirty, the outlook is grim and the lines have gone too far off the page.

Lastly, I hope we will consider the importance of reparations in America.

I understand them but I'm wondering just how long we, as Americans, need to continue making them? Is there a time-line on reparations? Could there be a time-line? How many times can I say "I'm sorry" and how many trillions of dollars do I have to spend until you believe me? Will I forever be condemned for my father's sins?

"And all the kings' horses and all the kings' men could not

put Humpty Dumpty back together again."

I hope we will have the courage, strength and time in our lives to put America back together again!